It Starts With Food Cookbook: A Beginners Guide To A 30 Day Paleo Whole Meal Plan- Discover How I Lost 75lbs and Enjoyed Life!

By Ben Williams

Copyright © 2014 by: Ben Monroe

All rights reserved. This book or any portion thereof may not be reproduced or used in any manner whatsoever without the express written permission of the publisher except for the use of brief quotations in a book review.

Disclaimer:

Note: This book is not authored by Dallas and Melissa Hartwig. This cookbook is authored by Ben Monroe and the recipes it includes were created based on food choices recommended in "It Starts With Food" The information provided in this book is designed to provide helpful information on the subjects discussed. The publisher and author are not responsible for any specific health or allergy needs that may require medical supervision and are not liable for any damages or negative consequences from any treatment, action, application or preparation, to any person reading or following the information in this book.

Alamance County Public Libraries
342 S. Spring Street
Burlington, North Carolina 27215

TABLE OF CONTENTS

About The Book .... -5
Introduction .... -6
Basics of Whole30 Diet –It Starts With the Food .... -9
Benefits of Whole30 Diet Plan .... -10
Beginners Guide To the Whole30 Diet -IT Starts With Food .... -11
How the Whole30 Diet Help To Reduce Weight .... -13
Basic Tips and Tricks to Help You Lose Weight in the Whole30 Diet .... -14
Meal Plan .... -15
   Day 1 Meal Plan .... -15
   Day 2 Meal Plan .... -20
   Day 3 Meal Plan .... -26
   Day 4 Meal Plan .... -33
   Day 5 Meal Plan .... -37
   Day 6 Meal Plan .... -43
   Day 7 Meal Plan .... -49
   Day 8 Meal Plan 54
   Day 9 Meal Plan .... -60
   Day 10 Meal Plan .... -67
   Day 11 Meal Plan .... -72
   Day 12 Meal Plan .... -76
   Day 13 Meal Plan .... -80
   Day 14 Meal Plan .... -86
   Day 15 Meal Plan .... -91
   Day 16 Meal Plan .... -95
   Day 17 Meal Plan- 100
   Day 18 Meal Plan 105

- Day 19 Meal Plan .... -111
- Day 20 Meal Plan .... -116
- Day 21 Meal Plan .... -122
- Day 22 Meal Plan .... -126
- Day 23 Meal Plan .... -130
- Day 24 Meal Plan .... -134
- Day 25 Meal Plan .... -138
- Day 26 Meal Plan .... -142
- Day 27 Meal Plan .... -147
- Day 28 Meal Plan .... -152
- Day 29 Meal Plan .... -157
- Day 30 Meal Plan .... -162

Shopping List .... -166

Thank You - - - - - - - - - - 168

Other Recommended Books - - - - - - - - 169

About The Book

The basic aim of writing this recipe book was to provide all people some delicious and mouth-watering Paleo (Whole30) recipes initiated towards a better and healthy life. If you want to become a Paleo Geek then this book is a gateway to your success. This potential diet changes the way you eat food for the rest of your life. There is a Whole30-day meal plan along with a shopping list, so that the transition goes smoothly.

So jump in for a better Paleo Diet (Whole30) experience.

Introduction

Welcome to PALEO (Whole30-diet cookbook). As per the name, this book is targeted towards all those people who want to follow a Paleo diet and see some result just in 30 days. Most of the people get frustrated just by thinking of the word "DIET". Unlike other weight loss program, Whole30 is not a diet; it is a lifestyle to follow.

My weight loss journey began during my professional days. I used to get hungry a lot. My coworkers always asked me for lunch I never refuse them, perhaps I was meaner with my meals; so I ended up taking about five to six meals a day. As a result, I got obsessed and my body fat blew up to 40 percent.

In 1995 frustrated with my obesity, I decided to compete in a marathon race about 25 miles every month. Still got no good results. Well, as time passed, I was deeply concerned about my obesity. In 2008, I decide to join a local gymnasium; I really worked hard doing weight lifts, cardio and performing gymnastic moves.

I used to do high intense exercise 4 days per week. In addition, for the rest of the days I ran 10 miles. I started excluding fats from my diet and started eating seafood, vegetables and fruits. I tried to stay away from junk as much as possible. As a result, I lost more than 20 pounds. However, exercising for more than a year could not possibly lower my body fat to more than 27 percent, which made me worried.

Well, I do want to feel active, and energetic so I kept my gym sessions going. As time passed, I started feeling a lack of stamina to take my gym seriously. I really do not want to end up adding up what I had lose after a year of hard training. That was the time I heard about Dallas and Melissa Hartwig's Whole30 program. Therefore, I decide to try it. I started my first Whole30 diet in 2010. Just after 2 weeks, I felt happier, and energetic.

After a few months of following Whole30 Diet plan, my annual blood report showed good cholesterol up and down. I started losing 5 pounds per month and continuing into the 15th month I had lost about 75 pounds. Therefore, I stopped when I felt I had reached my ideal weight. Now, I am happy and confident. I go about life with so much energy.

Being so inspired by the Whole30 program, I decide to meet the founders. Therefore, I attend one of their workshops and met them. I sure appreciate their knowledge to change the lives and presenting food in an easy way. Both of them really made the overall weight loss process easier. Been a follower, I decided to create a whole30 diet plan that would help people get the result I got while following the whole30 program. This book serves the reader well with that purpose. You'll discover lots of healthy and delicious recipes, **I have put together a lot of recipes that worked wonders for me!**

Basics of Whole30 Diet – It Starts With the Food

Well, sure it starts with the food. The Whole30-diet plan is the best and fast way to change your unhealthy eating and craving habits. It is gluten free, dairy free, soy free, sugar and alcohol free plan that is also known as Whole30 diet plan. Two diet founders Dallas and Melissa Hartwig, established this 30 day diet plan to change your life. According to them, certain foods like sugar, alcohol, grains, legumes and dairy have a bad impact on your body.

Most body weaknesses and overweight issues are related to bad eating habits. Our physicians, therefore, recommend certain eating habits to cure illnesses. In today's ever changing society we all are busy and want ease of access to everything. If you want a healthy life and want tasty food that is low in calories that contributes to weight loss and a healthier you, then Whole30-diet plan is just for you. About 90 percent of weight loss followers improve health and lose weight following diet plans.

Benefits of Whole30 Diet Plan

- Weight loss
- Improve body efficiency and performance
- Better sleep, fitness and health
- Feel active and happier in life
- Improve athletic performance
- Improve skin condition
- Make hair stronger and shinier
- Help getting rid of stress and anxiety
- Reduce bloating and gas
- Increase stamina and fitness
- Lower risk of diabetes, cancer and heart attack

Beginners Guide To the Whole30 Diet -IT Starts With Food

If you are a beginner then this guide will help you to follow a perfect Whole30-diet plan. It starts with food choices. You need to focus just on good food items for the entire30 days. You do not need to weigh the calories, or stress about weight measures. You just need to eat good food.

Food to eat

Fruits

Vegetables

Seafood

Nuts

Seeds

Healthy fat like lard, ghee, olive oil, nut oil

Lean meat

Meat from grass fed pastures

Food to avoid for 30 days

Dairy

Legumes

Grains

Processed food

Canned items

Sugar

Artificial flavors

Alcohol

Junk food

Deep fried items

How the Whole30 Diet Help To Reduce Weight

Paleo (Whole30) diet plan helps you lose weight naturally and without struggling a lot. The basic reason for weight loss are:

• You eat high nutrient food.
• You lose water retention.
• You get rid of certain allergies.
• Increased amount of fat and protein helps you burn fat stored in the body, which leads to weight loss.
• You feel satisfied, as the health meal help reducing hunger pangs.
• You maintain healthy blood sugar.
• Your body uses stored fat for energy instead of consuming carbohydrates and sugar.

Basic Tips and Tricks to Help You Lose Weight in the Whole30 Diet

- Drink plenty of water throughout the day.
- Eat simple food in small quantities.
- Don't be a couch potato and move frequently throughout the day.
- Say NO to beverages.
- Say NO to sugar and artificial sweets and canned food items.
- Avoid drinking water during meal

If you follow this tips, you would lose weight effortlessly and be a slimmer and sexy you.

Now, let's Begin Our 30-Day Meal Plan

My 30 Days Meal Plan

Day 1 Meal Plan

Breakfast

Sausage Stir-Fry Breakfast

Preparation Time: 20 Minutes
Yield: 4 serving

Ingredients

2 teaspoons of coconut oil
2 yellow onions, diced
1lb of sausages made from grass-fed, pastured meat (cow or goat preferred), cut into round shape
4 cups of broccoli

Preparation

Heat oil in a large skillet and then add coconut oil.
Add onions in oil and sauté for about 2 minutes.

Next, add the broccoli and reduce the heat, cover the pan with id and let it get soften.
Then add the sausages and stir-fry until brown.
Cook of about 5 to 10 more minutes and then serve.

Lunch

Roasted Cauliflower

Preparation Time: 25 minutes
Yield: 6 to 7 servings

Ingredients

8 cups of cauliflower florets
1 cup of olive oil
1 tablespoon of garlic and ginger
5 tablespoons of lemon juice
½ teaspoon of salt
1 teaspoon of black pepper
Chives for garnishing

Preparation

Preheat the oven to 375 degree F.
Take a frying pan and heat oil in it.
Cook cauliflower in the pan and season with salt and pepper
Next, add in the lemon juice, ginger garlic paste and stir occasionally.
Cook for about 20 minutes with the lid on.
At the end add the chives and serve.

Snack

Bacon and Dates Rolls

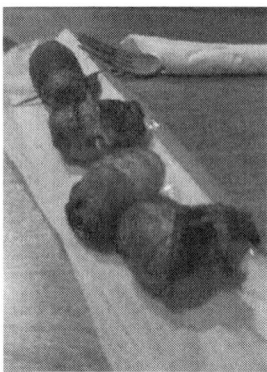

Yield: 2 Servings
Preparation Time: 10 Minutes

Ingredients

8 bacon slices, cut in half
8 large dates, pitted
8 whole almonds

Preparation

Preheat microwave at 400 degree F.
Wash the dates and take knife to open the dates, remove the seeds.
Stuff the date with almond, one each date.
Roll the bacon slice around the date, one slice per date.
Bake in oven for about 10 minutes serve and enjoy.

Dinner

Garlic Chicken

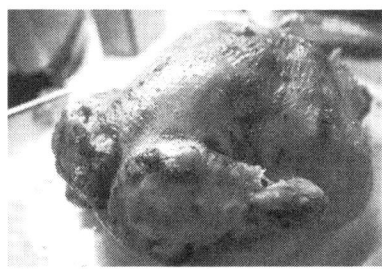

Preparation Time: 40-60 Minutes
Yield: 4 Servings

Ingredients

1 cup lemon juice
1/3 cup garlic paste
1 whole chicken, skinless
1 cup olive oil
Salt and black pepper to taste

Preparation

Preheat oven at 375 degree F.
Take a large bowl and combine garlic, lemon juice.
Rub the mixture over the chicken
Sprinkle salt and pepper at the end.
Let it sit for 30 minutes.
Then drizzle olive oil on top and bake in oven until golden brown.
Cover the chicken with aluminum foil so that steam softens the chicken.
Turn off the oven and after sitting for 10 minutes serve.

Day 2 Meal Plan

Breakfast

Salmon and Egg Scramble

Preparation Time: 10 minutes
Yield: 4 servings

Ingredients

1 teaspoon of coconut oil
4 organic eggs
3 tablespoons of water
4-6 Oz. smoked salmon, sliced, or broken into small pieces
2 avocados, sliced
Salt and black pepper to taste
1 green onion, chopped

Preparation

In a large skillet, heat the oil and sauté onion in it.
Take a bowl and whisk the eggs with water.
Then pour into pan to make an egg scramble.
Once the eggs cooked, add in the salmon and stir to make a fluffy omelet.
Sprinkle salt and black pepper at the end.
Pour the mixture into the plate and serve with the slices of avocado.

Lunch

Paleo Crab Cakes

Preparation Time: 20 minutes
Yield: 5 servings

Ingredients

2 organic eggs, whole
3 teaspoons of mustard
1 teaspoon of Worcestershire sauce
1/2 teaspoon of hot pepper sauce
2 teaspoons of lemon juice
2 teaspoons of seafood seasoning
Ground black pepper, (to taste)
1 pound of fresh crabmeat
1 cup of almond flour
½ tablespoon of red pepper
1 green onion
1-2 tablespoon of chopped parsley
1/3 cup of almond flour
Oil for greasing

Preparation

Preheat the oven at 375 degree F.
Grease the baking sheet with oil and set aside.
In a small bowl, whisk egg, then add mustard, lemon juice, Worcestershire sauce, seafood seasoning, lemon juice, hot sauce and black pepper.
Put the meat in a bowl and mix well.
Next, add into the bowl the flour, green onion, pepper and parsley, mix well and then make patties with the hand.
Bake the patties in the oven for about 25 minutes; remember to turn the side after 10-15 minutes.
Once, the crab patties are golden brown..
Serve and enjoy.

Snack

Roasted Pumpkin Seeds

Preparation Time: 15 Minutes
Yield: 2-4 Servings

Ingredients

2 cups Pumpkin seeds
Pinch of salt

Preparation

Take a baking tray and place parchment paper on it.
Remove the skin from pumpkin seeds and layer over a baking tray.
Bake in oven at 375 degree F for 15 minutes.
Sprinkle salt and enjoy.

Dinner

Paleo Salmon and Coconut

Preparation Time: 20-30 Minutes
Yield: 2 Servings

Ingredients

2 lbs. of salmon, wild caught
2 teaspoons of coconut oil
Pinch of sea salt and Black pepper, or to taste
6 mint leaves, diced
4 cloves of garlic, peeled, chopped and minced
1 lemon, zest
3 teaspoons lemon juice
2-3 cups of coconut milk
2 tablespoons basil, chopped

Preparation

Preheat oven at 375 degree F.
Place salmon on baking tray and bake in oven for about 15 minutes, until done.

Sprinkle salt and pepper over salmon.
In a medium frying pan, heat oil and sauté the garlic and add coconut milk
Let it simmer for 5 minutes.
Next, add lemon juice, basil, and lemon zest.
Pour this mixture over baked salmon.
Serve with mint leaves topping.

Day 3 Meal Plan

Breakfast

Paleo Pumpkin Muffins

Preparation Time: 30 Minutes
Yield: 5 servings

Ingredients

1-1/2 cups of almond flour
1-1/2 cups of pumpkin, cooked and puree
2 large eggs
1 teaspoon of baking powder
1/3 teaspoon of ground cinnamon
¼ teaspoon sea salt
1/2 cups raw honey
3 teaspoon coconut oil
2 tablespoons almonds, sliced or chopped
Coconut oil for coating and greasing

Preparation

Preheat oven to 350 degree F.
Coat the muffin tray with 1 teaspoon of coconut oil.
In a small bowl, add flour, pumpkin, eggs, baking powder, cinnamon, oil, salt, and honey.
Take an electric hand beater and make a batter.
Then add in almonds as well.
Pour the mixture into the tray and bake in oven for about 20-30 minutes. Once the top get brown and the muffins cooked thoroughly you can serve them and enjoy at breakfast.

Lunch

Paleo Chicken with Sweet Potato and Cauliflower Rice

Preparation Time: 20 minutes
Yield: 4 servings

Ingredients

1/2 cauliflower, cut into florets
2 chicken breasts, skin-less, bone-less and halved
2 tablespoons of paprika
Salt and black pepper (to taste)
1 tablespoon of coconut oil, divided
2 cups of sweet potato, cubed
1/3 teaspoon of ground cinnamon
1 teaspoon of ground nutmeg
Cauliflower greens, (optional)
2 lemons, juice, (optional)

1 cup of water, optional

Preparation

Place cauliflower into the food processor and pulse to get the form of rice grains.
Transfer to bowl and then add in the paprika, pepper and salt.
Heat oil in a skillet and stir the sweet potatoes, cook for a while then add nutmeg and cinnamon.
Once the potatoes get slightly tender, add the cauliflower mixture.
Add a bit of water so that the mixture does not stick
Cook for about 15 minutes at low heat with the lid on.
Take a separate pan and heat coconut oil and cook chicken pieces until brown.
Stir the cauliflower greens into the skillet and cook for about 5 minutes
Squeeze lemon juice and transfer to the sweet potatoes pan.
Give it a stir, so the ingredients combine well.
Then serve.

Snack

Cabbage and Salmon Snack

Preparation Time: 10 Minutes
Yield: 2 Servings

Ingredients

2 leaves of cabbage
3-6 oz. Smoked salmon
1 large red onion, minced
1 avocado, sliced
Salt and black pepper to taste
Olive oil for drizzling

Preparation

First step is to separate the leaves of cabbage.
Next place the cabbage on serving plate and top with salmon.
Next, layer the onions and sprinkle salt and pepper at the end.
Serve with the garnish of avocado slices

Dinner

Chicken Fajita Recipe

Preparation Time: 30 Minutes
Yield: 4 Servings

Ingredients

4 lbs. Chicken breast, cut in strips
3 onions, sliced
1 bell pepper, sliced
2 capsicums
6 garlic cloves, diced
4 tablespoons lemon juice
4 tablespoons of Cooking fat (lard)
1//3 cup vegetable stock

For toppings

Tomatoes, diced
Avocados, sliced

Preparation

In a small bowl, combine chicken, garlic, and lemon juice.
Take a frying pan and add lard, cook until oil come out.

Sauté onions in the oil and add capsicum and bell pepper.
Cook for 5 minutes and then add the chicken mixture.
Add a bit of vegetable stock and let it cook with lid on for about 20 minutes
Serve and enjoy.

Day 4 Meal Plan

Breakfast

Mushrooms with Eggs for Breakfast

Preparation Time: 15 Minutes
Yield: 4 servings

Ingredients

8 slices of bacon (save drippings)
5 organic eggs, beaten
3 medium onions, finely diced
16 wild mushrooms, finely chopped
Salt and black pepper to taste
4 tomatoes, chopped
3 tablespoons of olive oil

Preparation

In a medium skillet, heat oil and then add onions for Sautéing.
Cook for 2 minutes and then add in salt, pepper and tomatoes. Cook for another five minutes.
Now add in the mushrooms and bacons.
Stir twice and pour the eggs into the mixture.
Cook on low heat until the egg gets firm.

Serve the delicious omelet as a breakfast.

Lunch

Paleo Poached Whitefish in Tomato-Fennel Broth

Preparation Time: 20-25 minutes
Yield: 1-2 serving

Ingredients

2 tablespoons of olive oil
2 bulbs fennel, chopped
1 yellow onion, chopped
2 pounds of whitefish fillets
2 pinch saffron
2 tablespoons of fennel seeds
2 cups of diced tomatoes
1/2 cups water

Preparation

Heat olive oil in a skillet and sauté the onions.
Stir in the funnel bulbs and tomatoes and cook for 5 minutes until soften.
Next, add in the fish, fennel seeds, saffron and water.
Cook with the lid on for about 15 minutes until the water evaporates.
Then serve and enjoy.

Snack

Pork Rinds

Preparation Time: 30 Minutes
Yield: 2 Servings

Ingredients

2 cups Pork skin
Black pepper and sea salt

Preparation

Preheat oven at 375 degree F.
Place liner on baking tray and place the pork skins on it for baking.
Bake for about 25 minutes in oven.
Once, the rinds get crunchy form outside, sprinkle salt and pepper.
Serve and enjoy.

Dinner

Shrimp Fried Rice Recipe

Preparation Time: 20 Minutes
Yields: 2 Serving

Ingredients

1 yellow onion, chopped
2 cup shrimps
2 heads of cauliflower
2 organic eggs
2 cloves of garlic
4 tablespoons olive oil
Salt and pepper to taste

Preparation

Chop cauliflower in a food processor.
Next, heat oil in frying pan and sauté onions and garlic.
Add the cauliflowers and cook until soften.
Add shrimp to skillet and cook for additional 10 minutes.
Beat egg in a bowl and sprinkle pepper and salt.
Pour the egg into shrimp mixture and cook until eggs fluffy.
Serve and enjoy.

Day 5 Meal Plan

Breakfast

Breakfast Waffles

Preparation Time: 15 minutes
Yield 2 servings

Ingredients

2 bananas
4 organic eggs, beaten
2 tablespoons coconut oil
1 cup almond milk
½ cup almond flour
¼ cup natural shredded coconut
1/3 tablespoon cinnamon
Salt, just a pinch

Preparation

Preheat the waffle iron.
In a bowl, blend bananas, coconut oil, almond milk and eggs.
In a separate bowl, add in the almond flour, salt, shredded coconut and cinnamon.
Combine ingredients of both bowls. Mix well.

Once the batter is formed, pour the mixture into the waffles iron and cook until done.
Serve and enjoy.

Lunch

Cuban Peccadillo

Preparation Time: 40-60 Minutes
Yield: 2-3 serving

Ingredients

2 tablespoons of cooking oil (coconut or olive oil)
1-1/2 lbs. of ground beef
4 garlic cloves, minced
2 yellow onions, chopped
1 cup of tomato paste
12 pimento stuffed green olives
1 teaspoon of cumin
1 teaspoon of dry oregano
5 cups of beef broth
2 green bell peppers, diced
2 carrots, diced
12 bay leaves
Pepper and salt, to taste

Preparation

Heat oil in a skillet and add onion; sauté the onions.
Next, add ground beef and cook until turn golden brown.
Next, add the carrots and let it cook for five more minutes.

Add in the stock along with salt, pepper, and all the remaining ingredients.
Continue to cook for 30 minutes with the lid on.
Once the ingredients cooked, remove from heat and serve.

Snack

Spinach Crisps

Preparation Time: 15 Minutes
Yield: 4 Servings

Ingredients

2 bunches of spinach
3 tablespoons of olive oil
1/3 teaspoon of sea salt

Preparation

Preheat oven at 300 degree F.
Wash the spinach and remove the stems.
Place the spinach leaves on baking tray and bake in oven for about 15 minutes.
Once get crunchy sprinkle salt and drizzle love oil if like.
Serve and enjoy.

Dinner

Egg Drop Soup

Preparation Time: 25minutes
Yield: 3-4 Servings

Ingredients

4 onions, diced
2 tablespoons of olive oil
16 cups of chicken broth
2 teaspoons of ginger
2 teaspoons of tamari sauce
3 tablespoons water
8 organic eggs
5 stalks of celery
2 tablespoons arrowroot powder

Preparation

Heat oil in a pan and sauté onion and then add celery.
Add the chicken broth and ginger as well.
Cook until boil come. Then add tamari sauce as well.
Meanwhile, in same bowl, mix water with arrowroot powder and add to the cooking pan.
Beat eggs in a small bowl and add into the soup, once eggs get fluffy and cooked
The soup is done, serve and enjoy.

Day 6 Meal Plan

Breakfast

Paleo Sweet Potato Hash Browns

Preparation Time: 10 minutes
Yield: 4 servings

Ingredients

2 large sweet potatoes, peeled and grated
4 tablespoons melted cooking fat (lard)
2 green onions, chopped
½ teaspoon of ginger garlic paste (homemade)
Sea salt and black pepper to taste
1 cup chopped bacon for topping, optional

Preparation

Take a frying pan and sauté the onions in melted lard.
Add in salt and pepper.
Next, add ginger and garlic paste.

Cook for a few seconds and then add potatoes and cook until potatoes get tender.
Serve and enjoy with the topping of bacon pieces

Lunch

Cauliflower Fried "Rice" (Paleo)

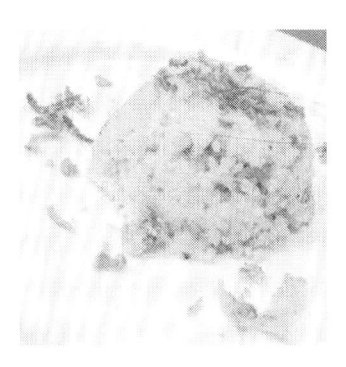

Preparation Time: 20 minutes
Yield: 3 serving

Ingredients

3 cups of grated raw cauliflowers
2 cups of frozen snow peas
1 cup of carrot, sliced
4 garlic cloves, minced
2 cups of onion, diced
2 tablespoons of olive oil
2 eggs, scrambled with 3 egg whites
2 tablespoons of lemon juice
½ cup of Vegetable stock

Preparation

First, heat oil in the pan and sauté garlic and onions.
Once the onions get transparent, add the snow peas and carrots.
Add in stock and cook for 10-15 minutes.
Once, the vegetables are cooked, stir in the eggs, lemon juice, and cauliflower.

Cook for about 10 minutes with the lid on so that steam cooks the ingredients properly.
Serve and enjoy.

Snack

Apple Bites

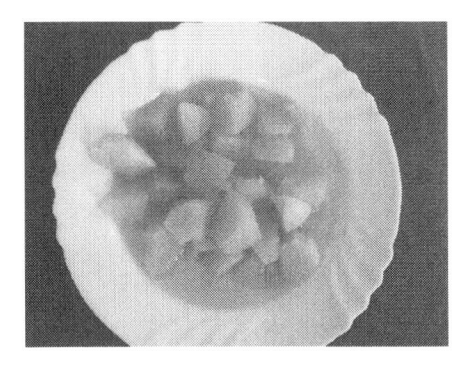

Preparation Time: 25 Minutes
Yield: 3 Servings

Ingredients

6 cups of apples, peeled and sliced
1 cup of honey
1/2 tablespoon of olive oil
Pinch of cinnamon

Preparation

Preheat oven at 350 degree F
Grease baking tray with olive oil.
Take a bowl and add apples along with the remaining ingredients.
Bake in oven until apples turns slightly brown.
Serve.

Dinner

Eggs and Steak Recipe

Preparation Time: 30 Minutes
Yield: 3 Servings

Ingredients

3 organic eggs
3 large steaks
4 tablespoons olive oil
Salt to taste
Black pepper to the taste
Paprika to the taste
1 teaspoon of ginger garlic paste

Preparation

First, season the steak with salt, pepper, paprika, and ginger garlic paste
Let it sit for 10 minutes.
In a frying pan, heat oil over low to medium flame.
Cook the steak for about 4 minutes per side. Place the steak in separate serving plate.
Add a bit more oil and fry the egg in the same pan.
Serve over steak and enjoy.

Day 7 Meal Plan

Breakfast

Paleo Zucchini Patties

Preparation Time: 5 minutes
Yield: 4 servings

Ingredients

4 zucchinis
4 green onions
5 organic eggs
Salt and pepper to taste
3-5 tablespoons of olive oil

Preparation

First, wash the zucchinis and then grate it with the cheese grater
In a small bowl, combine zucchini, eggs, green onions, salt and pepper.
Make patties with hand.
Next, take a skillet and heat oil in it.
Fry the patties in skillet.
Once the both sides cooked thoroughly serve and enjoy

Alamance County Public Libraries
342 S. Spring Street
Burlington, North Carolina 27215

Lunch

Pina Colada Chicken with Cauliflower Rice

Preparation Time: 30 minutes
Yield: 4 serving

Ingredients

12 ounces of chicken
4 tablespoons coconut oil (to sauté chicken)
1 cup of pineapple
2 cups of coconut milk
1 teaspoon of lime juice
3 garlic cloves, crushed
Pinch of cayenne pepper
1 cup onion, diced
2 green peppers, diced
1/2 red pepper, diced
4 carrots, grated
2 cups grated cauliflower
2 teaspoons of coconut oil
Salt to taste

Preparation

Heat 4 tablespoon of coconut oil in a skillet and add chicken to sauté.

Once the chicken color turns pink put pineapples, garlic, coconut milk, lime juice, cayenne pepper and cook on medium heat.
Once bubbles come turn at low.
In separate pan, heat the 2 tablespoons of coconut oil and put pepper, onions and carrots
Stir twice until it gets brown.
Now add cauliflower in the pan and stir in the mixture of other pan.
Cook for about 5 minutes, then serve.

Snack

Coconut Candies Paleo Style

Preparation Time: 15-8 Minutes
Yield: 2-4 Servings

Ingredients

4 cups almond flour
2 teaspoons olive oil
½ cup of honey
1 cup of nuts (mix nuts or any of your choice)
2 cups coconut flour

Preparation

In a small bowl, add almond flour, coconut flour, honey, olive oil and nuts. Mix well and make small balls with hands
Let it sit for few hours in refrigerator before serving.
It is a best sweet treat and alternative to artificial sweet candies and chocolate.

Dinner

Paleo Liver

Preparation Time: 25 Minutes
Yield: 2 Servings

Ingredients

2 large Beef Livers
4 large white onions, sliced
5 tablespoons olive oil
Salt to taste
Pepper to taste
1 cup coconut milk
5 tablespoons of water

Preparation

In a frying pan, heat oil and sauté the onions.
Once, the onions get translucent sprinkle the salt and pepper.
Add liver to separate pan and let it cook thoroughly.
Add a bit of water and cook with lid on, once the liver is cooked thoroughly serve into plate and pour the onion mixture on top.
Enjoy.

Day 8 Meal Plan

Breakfast

Walnut and Berry Pancake

Preparation Time: 10 minutes
Yield: 2 servings

Ingredients

3 cups of almond flour
Pinch of salt
2 organic eggs
3 teaspoons of walnut oil
½ cup of chopped walnuts
½ cup of blueberries
1 teaspoon of baking powder
Honey (optional)

Preparation

In a medium bowl, add almond flour, baking powder, salt and chopped walnuts.
In a separate small bowl, beat eggs and add walnut oil.
Combine ingredients of both bowl and then fold blueberries at the end.
Pour the spoon full of the mixture into the cooking pan to make the pancakes.
Once the top gets bubbly flipped to cook from the other side.

Once the pancake cooked thoroughly, serve with the drizzle of honey on top.

Lunch

Fish and Vegetable Curry

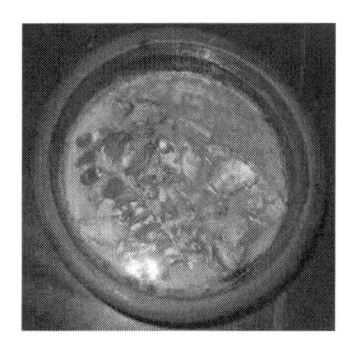

Preparation Time: 25 minutes
Yield: 2 serving

Ingredients

2 lbs. White fish fillets, cut it in a crosswise into 1/2" slices
2 cans unsweetened coconut milk
1 teaspoon of red curry paste
1 small red cabbage, sliced
Handful of cilantro, chopped
Salt and pepper to taste

Preparation

In a large sauté pan, pour the coconut milk and red curry powder
Cook for 5 minutes until the mixture get slightly thicker.
Add in the cabbage and let it cook until soften.
Add in fish at the end and cook until fish is ready.
Sprinkle salt and pepper at the end.
Garnish with cilantro and enjoy.

Snack

Banana and Strawberries Smoothie

Preparation Time: 5 Minutes
Yield: 4 Servings

Ingredients

6 oz. Fresh strawberries
2 large bananas
4 tablespoons of honey
3 cups of coconut milk
1 cup crushed ice

Preparation

Combine all the listed ingredients in blender and pulse until smooth. Serve into glasses and enjoy.

Dinner

Italian Steak

Preparation Time: 25 Minutes
Yield: 2 Servings

Ingredients

2 beef chunks, cut in slices
2 large yellow onions, sliced
1 teaspoon rosemary, dried
1 teaspoon oregano, dried
8 garlic cloves, chopped
Red pepper flakes
4 tablespoons of olive oil

Preparation

Preheat the oven at 360 degrees F
Take a bowl and combine all listed ingredients excluding steaks and olive oil.
Brush the steak with oil.
Place the steak in oil greased baking dish and pour the bowl mixture over the steak
Bake the steak for about 20 minutes in oven.
Remember to turn the steak after 3 -4 minutes each.
Turn the oven off and take the steak out. Cover all the ingredients with aluminum foil for about 10 minutes.

Slice the steak and serve immediately along with the ingredients as toppings.

Day 9 Meal Plan

Breakfast

Pina Colada Smoothie

Preparation Time: 0 minutes
Yield: 2 glass

Ingredients

2 bananas
1 cup of fresh pineapple chunks
2 tablespoons of coconut, shredded
2 cups of coconut milk
1 cup of crushed ice

Preparation

In a blender, combine all the listed ingredients and blend until smooth Once smoothie is ready serve in ice-filled glasses and enjoy.

Lunch

Chicken

Preparation Time: 30 minutes
Yield: 4 serving

Ingredients

2 shallots, roughly chopped
4 garlic cloves
2 Serrano chili peppers, sliced, stem is removed
1/3 cup of olive oil
8 boneless and skinless chicken thighs, cut from strips
1/2 teaspoon of sea salt
1/4 teaspoon of cayenne pepper
1 cup coconut milk
1/2 cup of almond oil
1 tbs. of lime juice
2 tbs. of fish sauce
1/4 tsp. of ground black pepper

Preparation

Blend garlic, Serrano, chili, shallots and peppers in a blender.
Add in the oil and make a paste.
Divide the paste into equal halves.

Put the chicken in zip lock bag along with salt, cayenne pepper and half paste; let it for marinating.
Meanwhile, in a saucepan add oil and remaining paste and cook for 5 minutes. Put all the remaining ingredients in it to form a thick paste. Add in the marinated chicken and lower the temperate.
Cook with the lid on for about 15 minutes.
At the end creamy consistency will form.
Serve and enjoy.

Snack

Cauliflower Poppers

Preparation Time: 15-20 Minutes
Yield: 5 Servings

Ingredients

1-2 heads cauliflower, break into bitable sizes
1 egg, beaten
1 cup bread crumbs, Paleo based
1 teaspoon salt, to taste
1 cup mint leaves
2 cups olive oil for deep frying

Preparation

Preheat oven to 375 degrees F.
Wash the cauliflower, then trim the core, and discard them.
Cut the cauliflower florets into bite size pieces.
In a small bowl, combine florets, sea salt, mint leaves and eggs.
Spread bread crumbs on a flat plate.
Roll the cauliflowers into breadcrumb.

Fry oil in pan and shallow-fry.
Serve and enjoy.

Dinner

Eggplant Balls

Preparation Time: 20 Minutes
Yield: 4 Servings

Ingredients

2 medium onions, diced
4 medium eggplants, diced
2-3 tablespoons water
2 tablespoons walnuts, toasted and chopped
½ teaspoon salt
4 cloves garlic, minced
4 tablespoons olive oil
2 lemons, zests
6 large eggs

Preparation

Preheat oven at 370 degree F.
Take a cooking pan and heat oil, then sauté onions for 5 minutes.
Add in eggplant and 3 tablespoons water, and cook for 15 minutes with the lid on.
Sprinkle salt and add walnuts.
Once the eggplants get soften, add walnuts.
After cooking for 5 more minutes, turn off the heat and let the mixture cool.

Next, puree the mixture in blender and then add all the remaining ingredients
Make the ball of eggplant mixture with hand and bake in preheated oven for about 15 minutes
Serve and enjoy.

Day 10 Meal Plan

Breakfast

Hot Breakfast Recipe

Preparation Time: 10 minutes
Yield: 2 serving

Ingredients

2 bananas, ripped
2 eggs
1 cup coconut milk
2 cups almond flour
½ teaspoon cinnamon
1 teaspoon coconut oil

Preparation

In a small frying pan heat coconut oil and place bananas for cooking. Let the bananas cook of about two minutes and then set aside.
In a small bowl, whisk egg along with coconut milk and cinnamon, pour the egg in the same pan and cook at low heat by adding almond flour
Cook for about 5 minutes by covering the pan.
Once, the egg mixture is cooked, serve into bowl with the topping of bananas.

Lunch

Salmon with Bacon & Orange

Preparation Time: 20 minutes
Yield: 4 serving

Ingredients

2 tablespoons olive oil for cooking
3 lbs. of wild-caught salmon filets
1 cup spinach, washed and stems removed
2 cloves of garlic, peeled and chopped roughly
2 blood oranges, peeled, cut in halves
2 fennel bulbs, roots removed, trimmed, and white parts sliced
2 large red onions, peeled and cut
Salt and black pepper to taste

Preparation

First, preheat the oven 375 degree F.
Cut the salmon in four parts with the skin.
Season the salmon with sea salt and pepper.
Bake in oven until golden brown.
Heat oil in a pan and cook spinach. Add in onions and garlic as well.
Next, add the fennel and oranges and slowly cook for 15 minutes.
After 15 minutes cover the pan and let the vegetable steam for 5 minutes; this will allow the liquid to evaporate as well.

Now place salmon on serving plate and top with the cooked mixture. Serve and enjoy with your favorite side servings.

Snack

Paleo Stuffed Eggs

Preparation Time: 10 Minutes
Yield: 1-2 Servings

Ingredients

2-3 eggs, boiled
½ teaspoon paprika
Pinch of salt, or to taste
1 cup snow peas, boiled
2 carrots, boiled and grated

Preparation

Boil water in a pan over high heat and boil the eggs.
Once the eggs are boiled, crack the shell and peel the eggs.
Cut the eggs lengthwise.
In a small bowl separate the yolks and add boiled carrots, snow peas, salt and paprika.
Mix well to form a paste
Fill the center of the egg white with the mixture and serve.

Dinner

Stuffed Potatoes

Preparation Time: 20 Minutes
Yield: 2 servings

Ingredients

4 large sweet potatoes, boiled
1 cup of black olives cut in cubes
1 cup green onion, chopped
1/3 teaspoons garlic and ginger paste
Salt and pepper to taste
1 cup chicken, boneless shredded and boil
Organic Butter (From Grass Fed Pastures)
2 Eggs, Boiled

Preparation

Preheat oven to 375 degree F
Peel and cut the boiled potatoes lengthwise, then center core them slightly with spoon.
In a medium bowl, combine boiled eggs, butter, shredded chicken pieces, salt, pepper, garlic, onion, potato pieces and olives. Combine all the ingredients well to make a perfect mixture.
Now bake potatoes in preheat oven for about 20 minutes
Serve and enjoy.

Day 11 Meal Plan

Breakfast

Fried Bacon with Apples

Preparation Time: 15 minutes
Yield: 2 servings

Ingredients

2 organic apples, peeled and sliced
4 cups bacon strips
1 tablespoon organic honey
1 tablespoon coconut oil
Half fried egg, optional

Preparation

Heat oil in a frying pan and cook bacon strips.
Transfer the bacon to plate and then fry apples in the same pan for about 10 minutes.
Add honey, once the apples get caramelized pour over the bacon and serve with half fried egg if liked.

Lunch

Chicken Recipe with Mushrooms

Preparation Time: 30 minutes
Yield: 4 serving

Ingredients

4 tablespoons of olive oil
6 ounce chicken breasts, pieces
2 cups of mushrooms, nicely chopped
1 cup of chicken broth +2 teaspoon coconut milk
1 teaspoon of oregano
Salt and pepper, to taste

Preparation

Heat oil in a skillet and add chicken breast, cook for about 10 minutes.
Then add in the mushrooms and cook for 5 minutes.
Pour the broth mixture and let the mixture boil.
Sprinkle oregano, salt and pepper at the end. Once thick gravy formed, serve and enjoy

Snack

Coconut and Pineapple Ice Cream

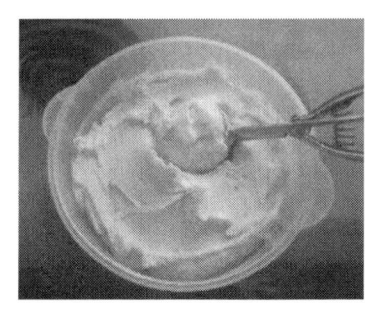

Preparation Time: 10 Minutes +Freeze In Refrigerator Overnight Yield 4 Servings

Ingredients

4 tablespoons coconut powder
2 cups of coconut milk
1/2 teaspoon honey
2 cups pineapple, cut in cubes

Preparation

Take a blender and combine coconut milk, coconut powder, honey and pineapple and blend until smooth. Pour the mixture into ice-cream maker to make a perfect ice cream. Pour the ice cream into a container and refrigerate overnight or for a few hours before serving

Dinner

Stuffed Eggplants

Preparation Time: 25 Minutes
Yield 2 Servings

Ingredients

3 egg plants, center cored
2 cups shredded chicken
1 green onion, chopped
½ teaspoons cumin
Salt, to taste
1 large green chili, chopped
2 teaspoons of lemon juice
1 tomato, chopped
2 tablespoons olive oil

Preparation

Heat oil in a pan and sauté the onions,
Then add salt, tomatoes, onions, pepper, lemon juice and cumin.
Cook until tomatoes get soften.
Now add the chicken and chili.
Cook for 10 minutes with lid on.
Now center core the eggplant and fill it with prepared mixture.
Bake in oven for about 20 minutes, until eggplants get soft.
Once done serve and enjoy.

Day 12 Meal Plan

Breakfast

Black Olive's Omelet

Preparation Time: 15 Minutes
Yield: 2 Servings

Ingredients

½ cup black olives, chopped
2 organic eggs, beaten
Salt, pinch
Black pepper, pinch
4 tablespoons olive oil
1 cup green onion, chopped

Preparation

Heat olive oil in a frying pan.
Next, sauté the onions in the pan for about 5-10 minutes.
Add olives into the pan and cook over low heat for about 5 minutes.
Sprinkle salt and pepper at this stage.
Whisked eggs in bowl and pour into pan.
Let eggs cooked from both sides. Once the omelet is cooked, serve and enjoy.

Lunch
Sausage Scotch Eggs

Yield: 6 Servings
Preparation Time: 35 Minutes

Ingredients

6 eggs
2 cups lean ground pork
Half teaspoon salt
Pinch of black pepper
2 tablespoons honey
2 teaspoons ginger and garlic, paste

Preparation

Boil eggs in a pot. Peel the eggs and then set aside.
Preheat oven at 375 degree F.
Boil the eggs in a pot filled with water
Line the parchment paper on the baking tray and set aside for further use.
In a large bowl and combine all the listed ingredients.
Now mix the ingredients well and make the round patties of meat.
Now place the egg in the middle of meat Pattie and roll over the eggs.
The large meatball shape will form.
Bake it in oven for about 25 minutes.
Then serve.

Snack

Baked Sweet Potatoes

Preparation Time: 15 Minutes
Yield: 2 Servings

Ingredients

4 sweet potatoes, peeled and cut into slices
Olive oil for greasing
½ teaspoon orange rind, grated
1 tablespoon honey
4 tablespoons of orange juice

Preparation

Preheat oven at 370 degree F
Take a bowl and combine potatoes along with remaining ingredients.
Then line in an oiled greased baking sheet.
Bake in oven for about 15 minutes
Enjoy

Dinner

Wings Stew

Preparation Time: 1 hour
Yield: 3-4 servings

Ingredients

6 lbs of chicken wings
1/4 cup of raw honey
2 tablespoons of garlic
2 tablespoons olive oil
sea salt and pepper, to taste

Preparation

In a bowl combine, garlic, honey, olive oil, salt and pepper.
Add in the wings and let the chicken wings marinate for few hours.
Now place all the ingredients in the crock-pot and cover the pot with lid.
Cook on medium heat for an hour
Once the wings done serve and enjoy

Day 13 Meal Plan

Breakfast

Cauliflower Fritters

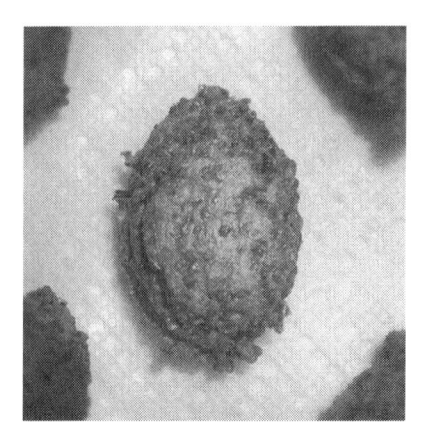

Preparation Time: 20 minutes
Yield: 4 servings

Ingredients

For coriander aioli

1 tablespoon of olive oil
2 tablespoons coriander, chopped
1 garlic clove, finely chopped
3 teaspoons of Lemon juice

Other List of ingredients

2 cups of cauliflower, finely diced
1 cup of broccoli, diced
6 organic eggs
2 tablespoons of coconut, shredded

Pinch of black pepper and salt
Melted Lard, for frying

Preparation

In a medium bowl, combine broccoli, eggs, coconut, cauliflower, salt and pepper.
Mix the ingredients well.
Heat lard in a frying pan and pour the mixture with the help of a spoon into pan to make fritters.
Fry from both sides for about five minutes each side.
Once the sides are golden brown the fritters are ready to be served.
For side serving, combine all ingredients of aioli and serve along with the main dish

Lunch

Stuffed Chicken

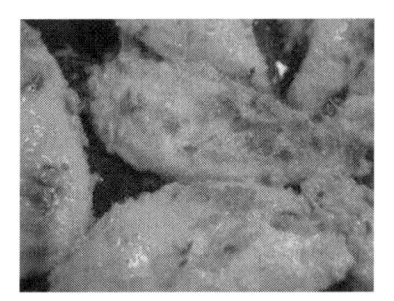

Preparation Time: 25-35 Minutes
Yield: 6 Servings

Ingredients

6 large chicken breasts
1 cup walnuts, chopped
4 Oz basil leaves
6 garlic cloves
4 tablespoons olive oil
4 teaspoons dried rosemary leaves
Sea salt and black pepper, to taste

Preparation

Take a food processor and blend walnuts, rosemary, basil, salt , black pepper and garlic.
Tender the chicken by beating it with a heavy object and then make a cut in the middle of the chicken; it should open like a book.
Place the batter inside the chicken and then roll lie flap
Make sure the seal is perfect and the mixture stays inside.
Drizzle olive oil on top of chicken and bake in oven for about 25 minutes
Serve once done

Snack

Homemade Organic Fruity Ice Cream

Preparation Time: 10 Minutes+ Freeze Overnight
Yield 2 Serving

Ingredients

1 cup raw strawberries
1 cup coconut milk
1 tablespoon shredded coconut
1 cup pineapple chunks

Preparation

Take a blender and blend all the listed ingredients in it excluding pineapple chunks.
Transfer the mixture to a container and add pineapple chunks at this stage. Then freeze overnight.
Once they are solid serve and enjoy.

Dinner

Stewed Pork

Yield: 6 servings
Preparation Time: 6 hours

12 ounces pork loin, boneless and shredded
5 large tomatoes, chopped
1 small green onion, sliced
2 cloves garlic, minced
2 teaspoons thyme leaves
2 jalapeño chilies, chopped
Salt and pepper, to taste
4 tablespoons of olive oil

Preparation

Heat the oil in a skillet and sauté onions in it.
Add all the listed ingredients in to skillet excluding pork loin.
Cook for 15 minutes.

Next, place pork loin in slow cooker and drizzle prepares mixture in skillet on top.
Cook for about an hour at high heat.
Once done serve and enjoy.

Day 14 Meal Plan

Breakfast

Spinach Omelet

Preparation Time: 15 minutes
Yield: 2 servings

Ingredients

2 eggs, beaten
2 tablespoons olive oil
½ teaspoon black pepper
Pinch of salt, or to taste
1 cup black olives, chopped
1 cup spinach, boiled and drained
2 green onions, chopped

Preparation

Take a non-stick frying pan and heat oil in it.
Sauté green onions.
Afterward, add black olives, spinach, salt and pepper.
Pour the whisked eggs on to frying pan over the vegetables.
Cook from both sides. Once done serve hot and enjoy.

Lunch

Mixed vegetable

Preparation Time: 50-60 Minutes
Yield: 6 Servings

Ingredients

2 cups carrots
2 cups onions, chopped
2 cups sweet potatoes, peeled and chopped
1/2 cup snow peas, washed
1 cup tomatoes
2 cups chicken broth
1 teaspoon cumin
½ teaspoon turmeric
1 cup olive oil, for cooking
Salt and red chilies, to taste
½ teaspoons Ginger and garlic paste

Preparation

Heat oil in a skillet and sauté the onions and garlic ginger paste in it.

Cook them until mushy, then add turmeric, cumin, red chilies, salt and cook for 2 minutes.
Next, add the potatoes, tomatoes, carrots, snow peas and broth.
Cover the lid and cook it for about 20 minutes.
Cover the skillet with the lid and cook for 25 minutes on low heat.
Once the thick gravy formed to serve and enjoy.

Snack

Beetroot Salad

Preparation Time: 5 Minutes
Yield: 2 Servings

Ingredients

1/3 cup lemon juice
1/2 cup tomatoes, halved
4 tablespoons fresh parsley
½ cup boiled sweet potatoes, diced
Salt and pepper to taste
1 cup beetroot, rinsed well and diced
1 tablespoon olive oil
1 tablespoon mint
½ cup black olives

Preparation

First boil water in pot and cook beetroots in it.
Once the beetroots get soft, drain the water and let it cool.
In a bowl, combine the entire listed ingredient along with the beetroots.
Serve and enjoy.

Dinner

Carrot Soup

Preparation Time: 20 Minutes
Yield 4 Servings

Ingredients

1 tablespoon olive oil
6 yellow onions, sliced
2 pounds carrots, thinly sliced
10 cups chicken broth
 Salt and pepper, to taste

Preparation

Heat oil in a cooking pot and sauté onions in it.
Once tender and soft, add carrots, salt and pepper.
Simmer for about 10 minutes and add broth.
Let the broth come to boil and then cook on low heat for about 20 minutes.
Before serving puree the mixture into blender and reheat to serve hot.

Day 15 Meal Plan

Breakfast

Almond Waffles

Preparation Time: 25-30 Minutes
Yield 3 Servings

Ingredients

1 cup of coconut milk
2-3 cups almond flour
½ cup almonds, crushed
2 organic eggs, separated
½ cup coconut oil
2 tablespoons raw honey

Preparation

In a small bowl, beat egg whites until they become foamy.
Take another bowl and beat yolks in it.
Then add in the honey, coconut milk, almond flour and crushed almonds.
Mix well and then add coconut oil.
Combine ingredients of both bowls to make a batter for waffles.
If the mixture is too thick, you can add more milk; if the mixture is runny, you can add a bit of flour to make it even.
Then pour into waffle iron.
Once done serve and enjoy.

Lunch

Spicy Crock-pot Chicken

Preparation Time: 50 Minutes
Yield: 4 Servings

Ingredients

4 chicken breasts,
4 tablespoons olive oil
Salt and pepper, to taste
2 cups chicken broth
4 tablespoons honey
2 tablespoons mustard paste

Preparation

Take a bowl and mix olive oil, salt, pepper, broth, honey and mustard paste.
Now place the mixture into crock pot along with chicken on top.
Cook on high heat for about 1 hour.
Turn off the crock-pot and let the steam out.
Open the lid and let it simmer for next 10 minutes or until gravy is formed.
Serve with cauliflower rice if like.
Enjoy.

Snack

Spicy Pineapples

Preparation Time: 20 Minutes
Yield: 2 Servings

Ingredients

1 large pineapple, peeled and cut into cubes
Cinnamon for sprinkling
Honey, as per taste

Preparation

Preheat oven at 350 degree F.
Next, line parchment paper onto baking tray.
Sprinkle pineapple with the cinnamon and honey.
Place in oven and bake for about 2 minutes
Once the color starts to change serve
You can also grill the pineapples on preheated grill instead of using the oven.

Dinner

Kale and Carrot Soup

Preparation Time: 35 minutes
Yield 6 servings

Ingredients

2 cups chopped onion
½ teaspoon salt
12 cups kale, cooked
4 tablespoons olive oil
2 red peppers, diced
4 tomatoes, diced
1/2 teaspoon cumin
6 medium carrots, diced
2 cloves garlic, crushed
1 teaspoon cayenne pepper
1 cup orange juice
1 sliced avocado, optional

Preparation

Heat the oil in a pan and sauté the onions.
Then add garlic, salt, red pepper, tomatoes, kale, cumin and cayenne pepper.
Cook for about 20 minutes with lid on.
Then afterward add the orange juice and bring the boil.
Serve and enjoy with the topping of avocado slices.

Day 16 Meal Plan

Breakfast

Coconut and Banana Smoothie

Yield 2 Servings
Preparation Time: 5 Minutes

Ingredients

2 cups coconut milk
2 bananas, peeled
2 tablespoons shredded coconut
Ice cubes for chilling

Preparation

Take a blender and combine all the listed ingredients in it. Pulse until a smooth mixture is formed.
Serve into glasses and enjoy.

Lunch

Cauliflower Soup

Yield: 6 Servings
Preparation Time: 1 Hour

Ingredients

10 cups chicken, broth
2 cups cauliflower florets, boiled
1/2 tablespoon red pepper
½ cup carrot
2 tablespoons of water
2 yellow onions, diced
4 cups sliced celery
4 lemons, juice
Salt and pepper, to taste
Olive oil, for cooking
Paprika, for garnishing

Preparation

Heat the oil in a large skillet and sauté the onions.
Next, add cauliflower and carrots and cook on low heat for 10 minutes.
Add a bit of water so that ingredients get soft during cooking.
Next add salt, pepper, celery, paprika, lemon juice and broth.
Cook on low heat for about 30 minutes with the lid on top.
Serve in to bowl once done.
Enjoy.

Snack

Stuffed Dates

Preparation Time: 10 Minutes
Yield: 6 Servings

Ingredients

1 cup pistachios, shelled and chopped
4 tablespoons orange juice, freshly squeezed
1 cup almonds
1 pinch of salt
24 large dates, pitted

Preparation

In a blender, pulse pistachios, orange juice, almonds and salt.
Pour the mixture in to the bowl.
Now take date and make a slit on one side to take off the seeds.
Now press the prepared mixture into dates.
Squeeze well, so that filling does not spill
Enjoy.

Dinner

Salmon Recipe

Preparation Time: 30 minutes
Yield: 6 servings

Ingredients

6 serving size salmons
3 red onions, sliced
2 teaspoons garlic paste
Salt and pepper, to taste

For sauce

1/2 cup olive oil
Half-cup Fresh lime juice
Pinch of cinnamon
Salt and pepper to taste

Preparation
Preheat oven at 375 degree F.
Layer the salmon on a foil and season with garlic, salt, pepper.
In a small bowl, combine listed ingredients of sauce, and pour it over the salmon.
Toss red onions on salmon and fold the foil.
Place it on baking tray.
Bake in oven for about 15 minutes.

Serve and enjoy.

Day 17 Meal Plan

Breakfast

Breakfast Orange Smoothie

Preparation Time: 5 Minutes
Yield About 4 Cups

Ingredients

1 cup frozen peaches, slices
1 cup carrot juice
4 cups orange juice
5 almonds

Preparation

Take a blender and pour all the listed ingredients in it.
Now blend until the pure is formed and smooth.
Serve into ice-filled glasses and enjoy.

Lunch

Snow Peas Sandwich for Lunch

Preparation Time: 20 Minutes
Yield: 6 Servings

Basic Ingredient

12 gluten free, paleo bread slices

Filling ingredients

6 tablespoons celery, chopped
4 cups tomatoes
3 cups potatoes
4 cups snow peas, boiled and crushed
Salt and black Pepper to taste

Ingredients for dressing

1 teaspoon mustard powder
1 teaspoon honey
1 cup mint leaves
1 teaspoon chili sauce
2 cups onions, chopped
4 teaspoons green chilies, chopped

4 tablespoons lemon juice
¼ cup water
Pinch of salt

Preparation

First, combine the dressing ingredients in blender to make dressing.
Take another bowl and combine all the filling ingredients.
Fill the bread slices with the filling ingredients and then bake in preheated sandwich maker.
Repeat this process until all slices are ready.
Serve with dressing.

Snack

Kale Drink

Preparation Time: 5 Minutes
Yield: 4 Servings

Ingredients

2 cups kale, washed and chopped
6 cups orange juice, freshly squeezed
1 cup coconut water
½ cup organic and Paleo based honey
1 teaspoon lemon zest
1 cup ice cubes, for chilling

Preparation

Combine all the listed ingredients in blender and pulse until smooth. Pure into serving glasses and enjoy.

Dinner

Cabbage Soup

Preparation Time: 40 Minutes
Yield 6 Servings

Ingredients

3 tablespoons almond oil
1 whole cabbage, diced
4 cups chicken broth
2 medium onions, chopped
1 cup coconut milk
1/3 teaspoon Red chilies
Salt and black pepper, to taste

Preparation

Heat oil in pan and sauté the onion, then add cabbage and cook for 5 minutes.
Afterward, add the chicken broth, salt, pepper and red chilies.
Once, the broth reduced, add coconut milk and give it boil.
Serve into bowls and enjoy.

Day 18 Meal Plan

Breakfast

Fruity Berries Muffins

Preparation Time: 20 minutes
Yield: 4 Servings

Ingredients

1 cup blueberries, peeled and diced
1 cup strawberries, diced
2 large cups of almond flour
1 cup of coconut, shredded
½ teaspoon cinnamon
2 organic Eggs, beaten
4 tablespoons honey
½ cup of coconut oil

Preparation

Preheat your oven at 370 degree F
In a small bowl, mix together almond flour, coconut shredded, cinnamon.
Take another bowl, whisk eggs, and then add oil and honey.
Combine ingredients of both the bowls and fold strawberries and blueberries at the end.
Pour the batter in muffin tin cover with liners.
Bake the muffins in oven for about 20 minutes

Once done and golden brown, serve and enjoy.

Lunch

Pumpkin Soup Recipe

Preparation Time: 35 Minutes
Yield: 4-6 Servings

Ingredients

4 green onions, chopped
2 garlic cloves, crushed
6 tablespoons olive oil
1/3 tablespoon red chilies, powder
1-1/2 kg pumpkin , peeled and cubed
8 cups chicken broth
4 cups coconut milk
1 cup water
Salt, to taste

Preparation

Boil the chicken broth in a skillet and add the pumpkins, cook until tender.
Now add in about 1 cup of water and simmer for about 10 minutes.
Heat oil in a separate pan and sauté the onions, salt,garlic and chili powder.
Once cooked, transfer this mixture to the broth mixture.
Cook on low heat with lid on for about 20 minutes.
When 10 minutes remain, add the coconut milk and once the thick texture is obtained serve hot into serving bowls.

Snack

Bacon & Guacamole Sammies

Preparation Time: 5 Minutes
Yield: 2 Servings

Ingredients

6 strips of thick-cut pastured bacon
1 cup Guacamole

Preparation

Layer the guacamole between two layers of bacon strip and serve on a plate. Enjoy.

Dinner

Broccoli Soup

Preparation Time: 30 minutes
Yield: 4 servings

Ingredients

2 tablespoons vegetable oil
10 medium broccoli crowns, chopped
4 vegetable bouillon cubes
2 medium onions, chopped
4 cups coconut milk
1/4 teaspoon Red chilies
Salt and black pepper, to taste
8 ounces shredded chicken cooked
4 cups water

Preparation

Heat oil in skillet and sauté onion in it.
Next, add onions, broccoli, water and bouillon.
Cook for about 10-15 minutes.
Once the ingredients get tender, let them cold and puree them in a food processor.
Now transfer them to cooking pot and heat the mixture, add the coconut milk, shredded chicken, salt, chilies and pepper.

Process in blender, once puree, transfer to cooking pan and cook for about 15 more minutes.
The serve and enjoy.

Day 19 Meal Plan

Breakfast

Paleo Cake for Breakfast

Preparation Time: 45 Minutes
Yield: 6 Servings and Above

Ingredients

6 dates, pitted and cubed
4 organic bananas, ripped and mashed
3 organic eggs, beaten
1/2 cup coconut oil
1 teaspoon vanilla extract
1 cup coconut flour
1 teaspoon baking soda
Pinch of salt
1/2 cup honey

Preparation

Preheat the oven to 300 degree F.
Take a food processor and purée the dates, bananas, eggs, coconut oil, vanilla extract, flour, baking soda, salt and honey.
Grease the cake pan with oil spray and pour the cake batter into the pan.
Bake it in oven for about 30 minutes at 250-300 degree F.

Once the cake is thoroughly cooked, slice, and enjoy at breakfast.

Lunch

Potatoes with Spinach

Preparation Time: 30 minutes
Yield: 6 servings

Basic Ingredients

1 clove of garlic, minced
3 cups boiled potatoes, cubed
1/4 teaspoon of cumin
2 onions, diced
Salt and pepper, to taste
1 teaspoon of curry powder
3 bunch's fresh spinach, chopped and boiled
6 tablespoons of olive oil
1 cup water

Preparation

Take a large cooking pot and heat olive oil in it.
Sauté the onions in it and add garlic, cook until caramelized.
At this stage add all the remaining ingredients and put the lid on.
Cook for about 25 minutes on medium low heat and enjoy

Snack

Paleo Bars

Yield: 6 Servings
Preparation Time: 10 Minutes
Freeze: Overnight

Ingredients

4 cups almonds
2 cups macadamia nuts
2 cups dates
2 cups peanuts
½ inch ginger, peeled and crushed
½ teaspoon cardamom, ground
1 cup cherries, dried

Preparation

Slightly Pulse all the listed ingredients in a food processor and press into baking sheet.
Refrigerate overnight and then cut into desired shapes for serving.

Dinner
Paleo Pork Chops

Preparation Time: 25 Minutes
Yield: 2 Servings

Ingredients

4 bones-in chops, lamb chops
2 large onions, chopped
Salt to taste
Pepper to taste
2 Cored apples, sliced
2 tablespoons coconut oil
4 tablespoons water

Preparation

Rub the chops with salt and pepper.
Heat coconut oil in a pan and fry the chops from both sides.
Once the chops get brown form both sides; set aside.
In same pan, add a bit more oil and sauté the onions and apple slices. Cook for about 10 minutes by adding a bit of water.
Once the apples get caramelized pour over the chops and serve

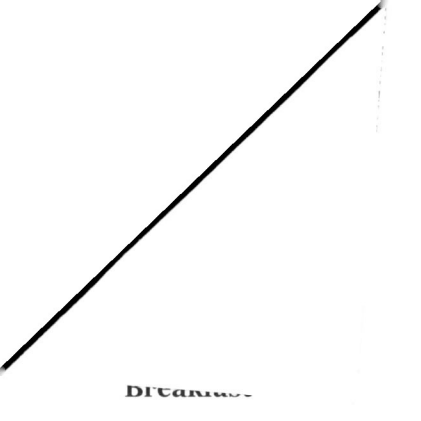

Blueberries and Banana Muffins

Preparation Time: 20 Minutes
Yield: 4 Servings

Ingredients

4 ripe bananas, mashed
1/2 cup blueberries
½ cup strawberries
½ cup honey
Pinch of sea salt
5 cups almond flour
4 tablespoons coconut oil

Preparation

Preheat your oven at 375 degree F.
Line the muffin papers on the muffin tray.
Now in a large bowl, combine all the ingredients excluding berries.
Make the batter and then fold in the berries as well.
Pour the mixture into the muffin tray and then bake in oven for about 20 minutes
Once done serve and enjoy.

Lunch

Spicy Chicken Soup

Cook Time: 30 Minutes
Yield: 2 Servings

Ingredients

2 cups carrots, sliced
16 ounces chicken breast, boneless and cut into cubes
½ cup chopped onion
4 tablespoons chili powder
½ teaspoon ground cumin
4 cloves garlic, minced
15 ounces chicken broth
2 cups tomatoes,
6 ounces green chilies
4 tablespoons water

For garnishing

2-6 avocados, sliced

Preparation

First, Heat oil in a cooking pot and sauté onions in it.
Add in tomatoes , garlic and chicken breast and cook for about 10 minutes.
Then add carrots and a bit of water , cover the pot with lid and cook for about 15 minutes.
Afterward, add chili powder, cumin, green chilies and broth.

Simmer for next 10 minutes with lid on.
Serve and enjoy with avocado slices.

Snack

Cucumber and Carrots Drink

Preparation Time: 5 Minutes
Yield: 4 Servings

Ingredients

6 carrots, peeled and cubed
4 cucumbers, peeled
½ lemon, juice
6 oranges, juice
4 tablespoons honey
1 cup ice cubes

Preparation

Blend all the listed ingredients in blender and pulse until smooth. Serve in to ice filled lasses and enjoy.

Dinner

Roasted lamb

Preparation Time: 2 Hours
Yield: 3 Servings

Ingredients

7 pounds Lamb, chops
2 lemons, zest only
1 cup Fresh Oregano
10 cloves Fresh Garlic, crushed
Salt, black pepper to taste

Preparation

Preheat oven at 370 degree F.
Combine oregano, pepper, garlic, lemon zest and salt in a small bowl and whisk well.
Rub the lamb well with the prepared mixture
Set aside for a while
Bake the lamb in oven for 40 minutes
Just before serving, turn on the boiler of the oven to make a crispy lamb roast
Serve and enjoy

Day 21 Meal Plan

Breakfast

Coconut Cookies

Preparation Time: 25 Minutes
Yield: 6 Cookies

Ingredients

2 cups Coconut flour
4 tablespoons organic honey
1 teaspoon baking powder
4 egg whites, beaten

Preparation

Preheat oven at 375 degree F.
Beat the egg whites in a bowl until they get foamy.
Then add in flour, honey and baking powder
Mix well.
Grease the baking tray with oil, and then pour the mixture into the tray in the form of cookies with the help of a spoon.
Bake in oven for 25 minutes.
Serve and enjoy.

Lunch

Pork Stew with Zucchini

Yield: 6 Servings
Preparation Time: 80 Minutes

Ingredients

2 pound pork loin, boneless and cubed
1 cup tomato, diced and drained
½ cup chicken broth
1 cup green bell peppers
½ cup chopped large onion,
1/ 2 tablespoon minced garlic clove
2 bay leaf
1 cup zucchini, thinly sliced
4 tablespoons water+2 tablespoons corn starch
Salt and pepper, to taste

Preparation

Take a crock-pot and combine all the listed ingredients in it excluding zucchini.
Cook on medium heat for one hours
Then open the crock-pot and add the zucchini
At this stage, you can discard bay bead and add cornstarch mixture
Cook on medium heat for next 10 minutes
Once thick gravy formed serve

Dinner
Kale Chips

Preparation Time: 10 Minutes
Yield: 4 Servings

Ingredients

4 bunches of kale
6 tablespoons of olive oil
1 teaspoon of sea salt

Preparation

Wash and remove the stem of kale.
Preheat the oven at 375 degree F.
Cut the kale in to bite size 5-inch pieces and layer baking sheet.
Drizzle oil on the top and toss well, le the kale bake in oven for 20 minutes.
Once crisp serve and enjoy by sprinkling salt on top.

Dinner

Battered Fry Chicken

Preparation Time: 30 Minutes
Yield: 4 Servings

Ingredients

4 chicken breasts, cut into cubes
½ cup coconut flour
4 eggs
2 tablespoons garlic powder
Salt and black pepper, to taste
Olive oil for deep-frying

Preparation

Take a bowl and add coconut flour, garlic powder, salt and pepper
Whisk eggs in a separate bowl and set aside.
Heat oil in a frying pan.
Dip the chicken pieces first in egg then in flour mixture and then fry in pan till golden brown

Day 22 Meal Plan

Breakfast

Pear and Bacon Bites

Yield: 4 Servings
Preparation Time: 25 minutes

Ingredients
8 slices bacon
4 pears, just-ripe
½ teaspoon cinnamon, ground
pinch salt

Preparation

Preheat oven at 375 degree F.
Place a large aluminum foil on a baking sheet.
Cut the bacon with a knife and then place it on a baking sheet,
Bake in oven for about 15 minuets
Next, cut the pears into slices and layer them in a cutting board
Now, roll pear with roasted bacon and sprinkle salt and paprika.
Place a toothpick between so that the ingredients bend together.
Serve and enjoy.

Lunch

Paleo Lamb Recipe With Cauliflower Rice
Yield: 4 servings
Prpartioon time: 1 hour

Ingredients

2 cups onions, chopped
2 cups tomatoes, chopped
½ teaspoon cumin
1 teaspoon red chili pepper
Pinch of salt, or to taste
2 teaspoons ginger garlic paste
500 grams ground lamb meat
½ cup olive oil
1 cup lamb broth
4 cups cooked cauliflower rice

Preparation

Heat oils in a skillet and sauté the onions.
Add tomatoes, ginger, garlic paste and then cook until tomatoes get soft and tender.
Then add cumin, salt, meat and red chilies.
Cook for about 10 minutes and then add broth.
Cover the skillet with the lid and cook for about 50 minutes.
Once, meat get tender and soft, serve with cauliflower rice.

Snack

Strawberries Drink

Preparation time: 5 minutes
Yield: 5 servings
Ingredients

2 cups strawberries
1 teaspoons honey
1 banana, ripped and peeled cup ice cubes

Preparation

Combine all the listed ingredients in the blender and blend until smooth
Pour in to glasses and enjoy

Dinner

Paleo Meatballs

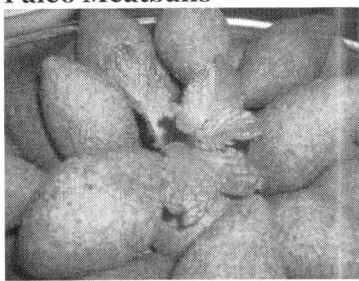

Preparation time: 30 minutes approx
Yield: 4 servings
Ingredients

800 pounds ground pork
4 green onions, sliced thinly
4 teaspoons coconut oil
2 teaspoons sesame oil
4 teaspoons fish sauce
6 tablespoons coconut, shredded
Sea salt, to taste

Preparation

Combine all the listed ingredients in a large bowl excluding oils.
Make a mixture and roll the mixture with hand to make balls.
Heat oil in a skillet and cook meatballs in skillet until brown.
Now place foil in a baking tray and cook in oven at 375 degree F for about 25 minutes.
Serve and enjoy with your favorite Paleo friendly dipping.

Day 23 Meal Plan

Breakfast

Berries Smoothie

Yield: 5 servings
Preparation time: 5 minutes

Ingredients

4 cups coconut milk
½ cup frozen bananas
2 cups frozen blueberries
1 cup frozen strawberries
1 cup ice cubes, optional
½ cup honey

Preparation

Pour all the ingredients in blender to make smoothie.
Pour into ice-filled glasses and enjoy.

Lunch

Eggplant Soup

Yield: 3 servings
Preparation time: 1 hour

Ingredients

9 cups chicken broth
4 eggplants, peeled, cubed
1 cup chopped onion
1/2 cup chopped green bell pepper
4 cloves garlic, minced
Salt and white pepper, to taste
Olive oil about 4 tablespoons

Preparation

Take a skillet and heat oil in it.
Sauté onions in oil and then add green bell pepper, garlic, salt and pepper and 1 tablespoon broth.
Let it simmer for few minutes.
Next, add eggplants and let eggplants get soften.
Once the mixture reduced serve in to bowl sand enjoy.

Snack

Salad

Ingredients

1 cup cucumber, diced
1 cup tomatoes, diced
1 tablespoon lemon juice
Salt and pepper
1 cup olives, boiled

Preparation

Combine all the listed ingredients in bowl and serve as a light low calories and healthy snack.

Dinner

Marinated Chicken Recipe

Preparation time: 20 minutes
Yield: 6 servings

Ingredients

600 grams chicken, boneless and cubed
½ teaspoon ginger, paste
½ teaspoon garlic paste
1 teaspoon Chili Powder
6 tablespoons mustard powder
Salt to taste
Black pepper, to taste
½ cup Lard
4 tablespoons lemon juice
4 eggs, beaten
Olive oil for frying

Preparation

Take a bowl and add chicken, garlic, ginger, salt, pepper and chili powder, and lemon juice.
Mix all the ingredients well excluding egg and mustard powder. Marinate for about 30 minutes
Dip the chicken first in egg and then in mustard powder.
Heat the lard in skillet and cook the chicken until get golden and tender.
Serve and enjoy.

Day 24 Meal Plan
Breakfast
Baked Egg

Ingredients

2 large Tomatoes
2 Large Eggs
Sea Salt & black pepper

Preparation

Preheat oven to 370 F.
Take a baking sheet and line it with aluminum foil.
Cut the top of tomatoes and centre cored then with spoon
Crack egg in tomatoes and bake in oven until eggs cooked properly.
Sprinkle salt and pepper on top and enjoy

Lunch

Tomatoes Pork Ribs

Preparation Time: 25 Minutes
Yield: 3 Servings

Ingredients

3 pounds pork ribs
5 Roma tomatoes, chopped
2 red bell peppers, chopped
4 small onions, roughly chopped
4 cloves garlic
1/2 tablespoon of cumin
3 tablespoons olive oil
6 sprigs of fresh rosemary
2 small bundle of fresh thyme, stem removed
Salt and black pepper, to taste

Preparation

Blend all the listed ingredients in blender excluding ribs in processor and make paste.
Rub the ribs well with the paste and marinate few hours.
Bake in oven at 400 degree F for about 40 minutes
Once done serve and enjoy.

Snack

Strawberry Pop

Preparation Time: 10 Minutes
Freeze Overnight
Yield: 2 Servings

Ingredients

2 cups strawberries
Cup coconut milk
2 tablespoons honey (organic)

Preparation

Blend the entire ingredient in blender and the pour into popsicles molds
Freeze until solid.
Serve.

Dinner

Pork and Squash Ragout Stew

Preparation Time: 1 Hour
Yield: 4 Servings

Ingredients

1-1/2 pound pork loin, boneless and cubed
2 cans tomatoes, un-drain
1 cup acorn squash, peeled
1 cup chopped onions
1/2 cup green bell peppers
1 teaspoons garlic, minced
Salt and pepper, to taste

Preparation

Combine all the listed ingredients in the crock-pot and cook for about 60 minutes at high heat
Once meat get tender let the mixture simmer for additional 10 minutes
Once stew is ready, serve.

Day 25 Meal Plan

Breakfast

Toast Casserole

Preparation Time: 40 Minutes
Yield: 4 Servings

Ingredients

Half loaf Paleo Bread, cut into 1-inch cubes
½ cup frozen blueberries
3 large eggs
1/2 cup coconut milk
¼ cup honey
½ teaspoon ground cinnamon
½ tablespoon vanilla extract

Preparation

Take a baking sheet and place bred pieces in it.
Take a medium bowl and mix eggs, milk, vanilla, and cinnamon.
Pour egg mixture over bread along with blueberries.
Bake in oven at 3755 degree F for about 30 minutes.
Serve and enjoy.

Lunch

Dried Beef and Onion Gravy

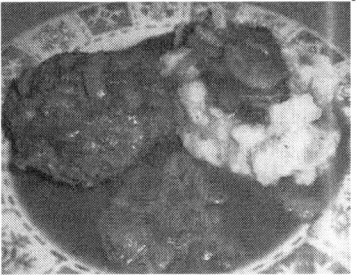

Yield: 8 Servings
Preparation Time: 1 Hour

Ingredients

10 ounces coconut milk
2 packages dried beef, chopped
2 cups thinly sliced green onions
6 tablespoons dried onion flakes
2 teaspoons garlic
Salt and pepper to taste

Preparation

Let the milk simmer in crock-pot.
Add in dried beef.
Mix the remaining ingredients in bowl and pour into the crock-pot.
Serve and enjoy,

Snack

Paleo Tuamole

Preparation Time: 5 Minutes
Yield: 4 Servings

Ingredients

3 avocados, mashed
3 limes, squeezed
1 cans of tuna, drained
1 cup of tomatoes, chopped
1 tablespoon of walnuts
Salt and ground black pepper, to taste

Preparation

Combine all the listed ingredients in the bowl and then serve. Enjoy.

Dinner

Dinner Time Egg and Bacons

Preparation Time: 10 Minutes
Yield: 2 Servings

Ingredients

2 roasted sweet potato, peeled
2 tablespoons olive oil
2 eggs

Toppings

1 cup Avocado
3 cups Bacon
½ cup jalapeño rings

Preparation

Heat oil in skillet and add precooked sweet potatoes.
Once, the potatoes get caramelized transfer to serving plates.
Fry egg in same skillet and add bacons as well
Pour it over potatoes
Serve.

Day 26 Meal Plan

Breakfast

Paleo Coconut Almond Drink

Yield: 4 Servings
Preparation Time: 5 Minutes
Ingredients
2 cups coconut milk
2 teaspoons cashew
4 bananas
2 dried dates
1 tablespoons honey

Preparation

Combine all the listed ingredients in the blender and make smoothie. Serve in to ice filled glasses and enjoy.

Lunch

Cream of Mushroom Soup

Yield: 5 Servings
Preparation Time: 30 Minutes

Ingredients

10 cups chicken broth
1 pound mushrooms, sliced
2 cups chopped onion
4 cups coconut milk, divided
2 tablespoons cornstarch +2 tablespoons water
Salt and pepper, to taste
4 tablespoons olive oil

Preparation

Take large bowl heat oil in it and sauté the onions.
Then add chicken broth and let the boil come.
Next add mushrooms and cook until they get tender.
Next add in coconut milk and cornstarch mixture
Cook for about 15 more minutes, and then serve by sprinkling salt and pepper on top. Enjoy this heart soup at lunchtime.

Snack

Carrots Chips

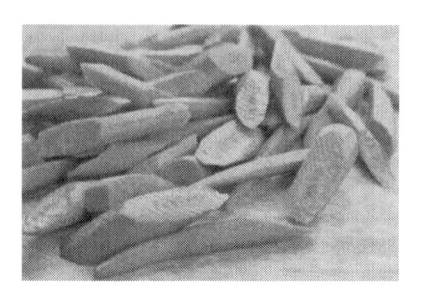

Preparation Time: 10 Minutes
Yield: 6 Servings

Ingredients

4 large carrots, cut length wise
2 tablespoons of olive oil
½ teaspoon of sea salt

Preparation

Wash carrots.
Preheat oven at 400 degree F.
Layer carrots on baking tray.
Preheat oven at 400 degree F.
Drizzle oil over carrots and bake in oven for about 10-15 minutes
Once crispy serve.

Dinner

Eggplants With Cauliflower Rice

Preparation Time: 40 minutes
Yield 5 Servings

Ingredients

6 cups chicken broth
2 cups coarsely chopped onions
4 tablespoons of olive oil
4 cups eggplants, cut in cubes
2 garlic, minced
1 teaspoons ground cumin
2 teaspoons curry powder
1 cup coconut milk
Salt and pepper, to taste
Cooked cauliflower rice, optional and for side servigns

Preparation

Heat oil in a pot and sauté onions, then add cumin, curry powder, salt and pepper.

Now add broth and let the boil come.
Add in the eggplants and cover the lid let it cook for 50-60 minutes at low heat until eggplants are cooked
Serve with cauliflower rice if liked
Cook for another 10 minutes and once the soup is ready, serve.

Day 27 Meal Plan

Breakfast

Raspberries Pancakes

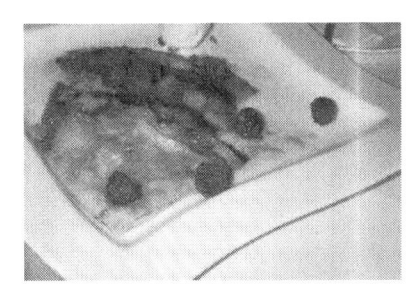

Preparation Time: 15 minutes
Yield: 2 Servings

Ingredients

2 cups of coconut flour
2 cups almond flour
Pinch of salt
2 organic eggs
2 teaspoons of walnut oil
1 cup raspberries
1 teaspoons baking powder
Honey (optional)

Preparation

Mix the coconut flour, almond flour, salt, baking powder in a bowl.
Take another bowl and mix reaming ingredients
Combine ingredients of both bowls to make a batter.
Pour the spoon full of the mixture into preheated greased pan to make the pancakes.
Once the top gets bubbly flip to cook other side.
Serve with drizzle of honey.

Lunch

California, Kale and Sweet Potatoes

Preparation Time: 50 Minutes
Yield: 4 Servings

Ingredients

1 large cauliflower, cut and cubed
5 sweet potatoes, baked
1 cup kale, chopped
4 bell peppers, chopped
3 small onions, chopped
1 cup coconut oil
1 tablespoon ground cumin
1 teaspoon ground coriander
3 lemon juice, squeezed
Sea salt & pepper, to taste
4 ripe avocados sliced
3 tablespoons of water

Preparation

Preheat the oven at 400 degree F.
Bake the potatoes in oven for about 30 minutes.
Take a large pot and heat oil init
Add bell pepper, onions, salt and black pepper,
Next, add kale and cook until ingredients get tender.

Next add in cauliflower and water, let it cook with lid on for 20 minutes. At the very end add the baked potatoes and squeeze limejuice on top. Let it simmer and then serve

Snack

Watermelon Drink

Preparation Time: 5 Minutes
Yield: 6 Servings

Ingredients

6 cups watermelon
2 limes, juice only
1/2 cup crushed ice cubes

Preparation

Combine the entire ingredient in the blender and blend until juice. Serve into glasses and enjoy

Dinner

Sweet and Sour Chicken

Preparation Time: 20 minutes
Yield: 5 Servings

Ingredients

3 chicken breasts
4 rings of pineapple
1 tomato
2 tablespoons lime juice
Salt and pepper
4 tablespoons olive oil
4 tablespoons of water

Preparation

Heat oil in skillet and cook until brown.
Sprinkle salt, pepper and water cook with the lid on for about 10 minutes.
Once the steam cooks chicken and make it soft.
Grill the pineapples on grill and then add to chicken.
Next, add limejuice, tomatoes and cook for 10-15 minutes at medium heat.
Once done serve and enjoy.

Day 28 Meal Plan

Breakfast

Egg White Omelet

Preparation time: 15 minutes
Yield: 4 servings

Ingredients

6 eggs whites
1 cup mushrooms chopped
1 tablespoon coconut milk
1 cup baby spinach, chopped
Salt and pepper to taste
½ cup green onions, chopped
1 tablespoon olive oil for frying

Preparation

Beat the eggs and combine mushrooms, coconut milk, spinach, salt, pepper, green onions in it.
Heat oil in a skillet and pour the mixture into the pan.
Let it cook for 5 minutes each side until eggs get firm.
Serve and enjoy.

Lunch

Seafood Soup Recipe

Yields 4-6 Servings
Preparation Time: 25 Minutes

Ingredients

4 tablespoons coconut oil,
1 white onion, diced
8 carrots, peeled and diced
3 garlic cloves, minced
2 teaspoons thyme, dried
½ teaspoon dried parsley
20 ounces mushrooms, sliced and then chopped
20 cups chicken broth
11 ounces coconut milk
2 ounces mushrooms, broken into pieces
3 cups chicken, shredded
1 cup frozen snow peas
sea salt & pepper to taste

Preparation

Heat oil in a skillet and add carrots, garlic, salt and pepper.
Let the ingredients cook for 10 minutes and then add thyme, parsley, mushrooms and coconut milk.

Let the boil come and then stir in chicken and snow peas, let it cook for 20 minutes and then serve.

Snack

Pineapple Pop

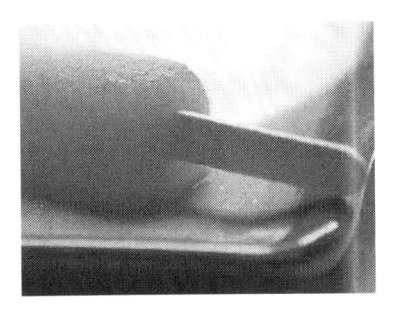

Preparation Time: 10 Minutes
Freeze Overnight
Yield 2 Servings

Ingredients

3cups pineapple chunks
2 cups pineapple juice
2 tablespoons organic paleo based honey

Preparation

Blend all the ingredients in blender and pour the mixture in to Popsicle molds
Freeze overnight, then serve, and enjoy.

Dinner

Pizza Recipe

Preparation Time: 10 Minutes
Yield: 3 Servings

Ingredients

3 large eggs, beaten
4 tablespoons marinara sauce
2 Paleo based muffins, split and toasted
4 slices pepperoni

Preparation

Preheat oven at 375 degree F.
Heat oil in skillet and scramble egg in it.
Add 4 slices of pepperoni as well.
Spread the marinara sauce on muffin and top with the eggs.
Broil in oven until melts.
Once done serve and enjoy.

Day 29 Meal Plan

Breakfast

Breakfast Tacos

Preparation Time: 15 minutes
Yield: 2 servings

Ingredients
4 paleo based tortillas
2 tablespoons salsa
2 eggs
Salt and pepper

Preparation

First, top tortilla with salsa.
Heat oil in skillet and cook eggs to make scramble.
Divide the scramble egg mixture between the tacos.
Serve and enjoy.

Lunch

Tomato Soup

Preparation Time: 35minutes
Yield: 5 Servings

Ingredients

2 tablespoons olive oil
2 teaspoons minced garlic
1 cup minced onion
1 cup tomato paste (you can make it at home my grinding the fresh tomatoes in blender)
2 liter chicken stock
½ cup diced tomatoes
3 teaspoons dried basil
½ teaspoon dried marjoram
1 bay leaf
½ teaspoon dried oregano
1/3 teaspoon dried thyme
Salt and pepper

Preparation

Heat oil in a skillet and sauté onions in it.
Once onions are translucent add garlic, tomatoes paste and cook for 5 minutes.

Add in the stock, marjoram, thyme, basil, oregano, bay leaf and diced tomatoes.
Bring the mixture to a boil and then cook for 30 minutes at low heat with lid on.
Once done serve and enjoy.

Snack

Apple-Lemon Slush

Preparation Time: 5 minutes
Yield: 2 Servings

Ingredients

1 cup crushed ice
2 cups fresh apple juice
4 tablespoons lemon juice

Preparation

Take a blender and purée all the ingredients. Then blend until it become slushy. Enjoy.

Dinner

Stuffed Mushrooms

Preparation Time: 5 Minutes
Yield: 2 Servings

Ingredients

4 potatoes, peeled and boiled
6 cups mushrooms
6 mint leaves
Half teaspoons of salt
Pinch of black pepper

Preparation

Heat water in pot and boil potatoes in it
Once the potatoes soften, drain the water and let them cool. Peel off the skin of potatoes and then mix in with mint leaves, salt and pepper in a small bowl.
Stuff the center core mushroom with the mixture and bake in preheated oven at 300 degree for about 20 minutes
Serve and enjoy.

Day 30 Meal Plan

Breakfast

Two Ingredients Pancakes

Preparation Time: 20 Minutes
Yield: 2 Servings

Ingredients

4 large organic eggs
3 bananas
1 teaspoon of baking soda

Preparation
Beat eggs with hand beater and add mashed bananas. Beat slightly to make a paste and add baking powder. Heat oil in pan and cook the pancake, serve and enjoy.

Lunch

Picnic Stew

Yields: 6 servings
Preparation Time: 50 minutes

Ingredients

12 ounces beef, cubed
1 cup sweet potatoes, cube
1 can tomatoes, cubed
2 large onions
½ cup olive oil
2 red bell peppers
6 cups water
4 cloves garlic, minced
2 teaspoons red chili powder
4 teaspoons lemon juice
Salt and pepper, to taste
Paleo bread, side serving

Preparation

Heat oil in crock-pot and add beef, potatoes, tomatoes, onions, bell pepper water, garlic, chili powder, lemon, salt and pepper.
Cook on high heat for about 40 minutes until thick gravy formed
Serve with paleo bread if liked.

Snacks

Chunky Paleo Guacamole

Preparation Time: 35 Minutes
Yield: 4 servings

Ingredients

4 avocados, peeled and pitted
2 limes, juiced
2 jalapeno peppers, diced
2 clove garlic's, minced
2 small onions, minced
2 tomatoes, diced
1 tablespoon of fresh cilantro, chopped
salt and ground black pepper to taste

Preparation

Take a bowl, and add in avocados and squeeze lime juice on top.
Now, mash the avocados by fork.
Add in the jalapeno, garlic, onion, tomatoes, cilantro, salt, pepper and mix well. Serve and enjoy.

Dinner

Beef With Brussels Sprouts

Preparation Time: 25 Minutes
Yield: 4 Servings

Ingredients

2 tablespoons coconut oil
2 tablespoons chopped onion
1 teaspoon ginger and garlic, paste
½ cup grated sweet potato, peeled and grated
6 ounces of ground beef
3 ounces of Brussels sprouts, shredded
4 eggs, cooked as per liking (1 per serving)

Preparation

Heat the oil in skillet and sauté onions in it.
Then add potatoes and cook for few minutes.
Once potatoes are tender, add the ginger garlic paste.
Give it a stir and add Brussels sprouts.
Add water to pan and cook on low heat for about 30 minutes.
Top with fried egg and enjoy.

Shopping List

Oils	Nuts, Seeds	Spices And Herbs	Meat	Sea Food	Vegetables	Fruits	Others
Coconut oil Olive oil Almond oil Lard Walnut oil Sesame oil	Almonds Dates Mix nuts Walnuts Pistachio Peanuts Macadamia nuts cashew	Salt Black pepper mustard Worcestershire sauce hot pepper sauce seafood seasoning red pepper parsley pumpkin seeds mint leaves basil baking powder cinnamon paprika oregano cumin bay leaves dried arrowroot powder cilantro rosemary cumin coriander thyme turmeric	Sausages Bacon Chicken Pork skin Beef Steak Lamb chops Pork ribs Pork lion	Salmon Crab White fish fillets Shrimp	Yellow onions Broccoli Cauliflower Ginger Garlic Chives Lemon Avocados Green onions Pumpkin Sweet potatoes Cabbage Bell pepper Capsicum Mushrooms Tomatoes Fennel Green olives Carrots Bell pepper Celery jalapeño rings Spinach Snow peas Zucchini	Coconut Apples Pineapples Blueberries Strawberries Raspberries Bananas Oranges Peaches Cherries Watermelons	Water Almond flour Honey Vegetable stock marinara sauce Almond milk Chicken broth red curry paste eggs coconut milk paleo bread fish sauces Paleo bread crumbs guacamole vanilla extracts Paleo bread corn starch lamb broth

				Eggplants Mushrooms Black olives Beetroots Kale Cucumber brown lentils squash white onions		

Thank You

If you Follow the ultimate guideline provided in the It Starts With Food By Dallas & Melissa, And some of the Healthy and Delicious recipes For 30 Days. You are going to be seeing great results in your body and health in just 30 days, because it is proven to work.

If you enjoyed the recipes in this book, please take the time to share your thoughts and post a positive review with 5 star rating on Amazon, it would encourage me and make me serve you better. It'd be greatly appreciated!

If you have any question or anything at all you want to know about this program, you can hit me up via mail thru challymartin@gmail.com I am always there to help you.

THANK YOU!!

Other Health Related Books You Would Like

It Starts With Food: Discover the Whole30 and Change Your Life in Unexpected Ways! By Melissa & Dallas – NewYork Times Bestseller, Get it Here>> **http://amzn.to/1pwksD7**

Other Health Related Books You Would Like

BOOKS BY BESTSELLING AUTHORS

My 10 Day Green Smoothie Cleanse Protein Recipes: 51 Clean Meal Recipes to help you After the 10 Day Smoothie cleanse!

The 10 Days Green Smoothie Cleanse is a Phenomenal Program created to help people lose weight in 10 Days. This program is so powerful and life changing, that lots of people have achieved weight loss.

However, it is sometimes difficult to maintain the weight loss after the 10 day green smoothie cleanse, and that's why we have prepared high-protein meals to Assist with weight loss after the cleanse. In this Book you'll discover lots of High protein recipes that are healthy, clean, and delicious!

Get it HERE>> http://www.amazon.com/Green-Smoothie-Cleanse-Protein-Recipes-ebook/dp/B00KDQZH2C

The Tapping Solution for Weight Loss and Body Confidence is a powerful system that releases the emotions and beliefs that hold us back from loving our bodies. I use tapping on a regular basis and have personally benefitted from this powerful method. It's one of the most important practices in my healing arsenal.

Get The *The Ultimate Tapping Solution Guide: Using EFT to tap your way to WEIGHT LOSS, Wealth and Build Body Confidence for Women*

Click Here>> Amazon U.S Link>> http://www.amazon.com/Ultimate-Tapping-Solution-Guide-Confidence-ebook/dp/B00K6JB97S

Books on Health & Fitness Diets

RECOMMENDED BOOK FOR WEIGHT LOSS AND DIET:

My 10-Day Smoothie Cleanse & Detox Diet Cookbook: Burn the Fat, Lose weight Fast and Boost your Metabolism for Busy Mom, Restart your life with this cookbook and experience an amazing transformation of your body and your health. I am really excited for you!

CLICK HERE TO BUY: http://www.amazon.com/10-Day-Detox-Diet-Cookbook-Metabolism-ebook/dp/B00IRE3CV0

Get this bestselling Grain Brain Book- **My brain against all grain Cookbook: 61 Easy-to-make Healthy Foods that would help you stick to the Grain-Brain-free Diet!**

Discover The Surprising Truth about Wheat, Carbs, and Sugar--Your Brain's Silent Killers

Amazon US Link: http://www.amazon.com/dp/B00J9DX3X0

Amazon UK Link: http://www.amazon.co.uk/dp/B00J9DX3X0

The Coconut Diet Cookbook: Using Coconut Oil to Lose weight FAST, Supercharge Your Metabolism & Look Beautiful!

Link http://www.amazon.com/dp/B00K1II0GS

Alamance County Public Libraries
342 S. Spring Street
Burlington, North Carolina 27215